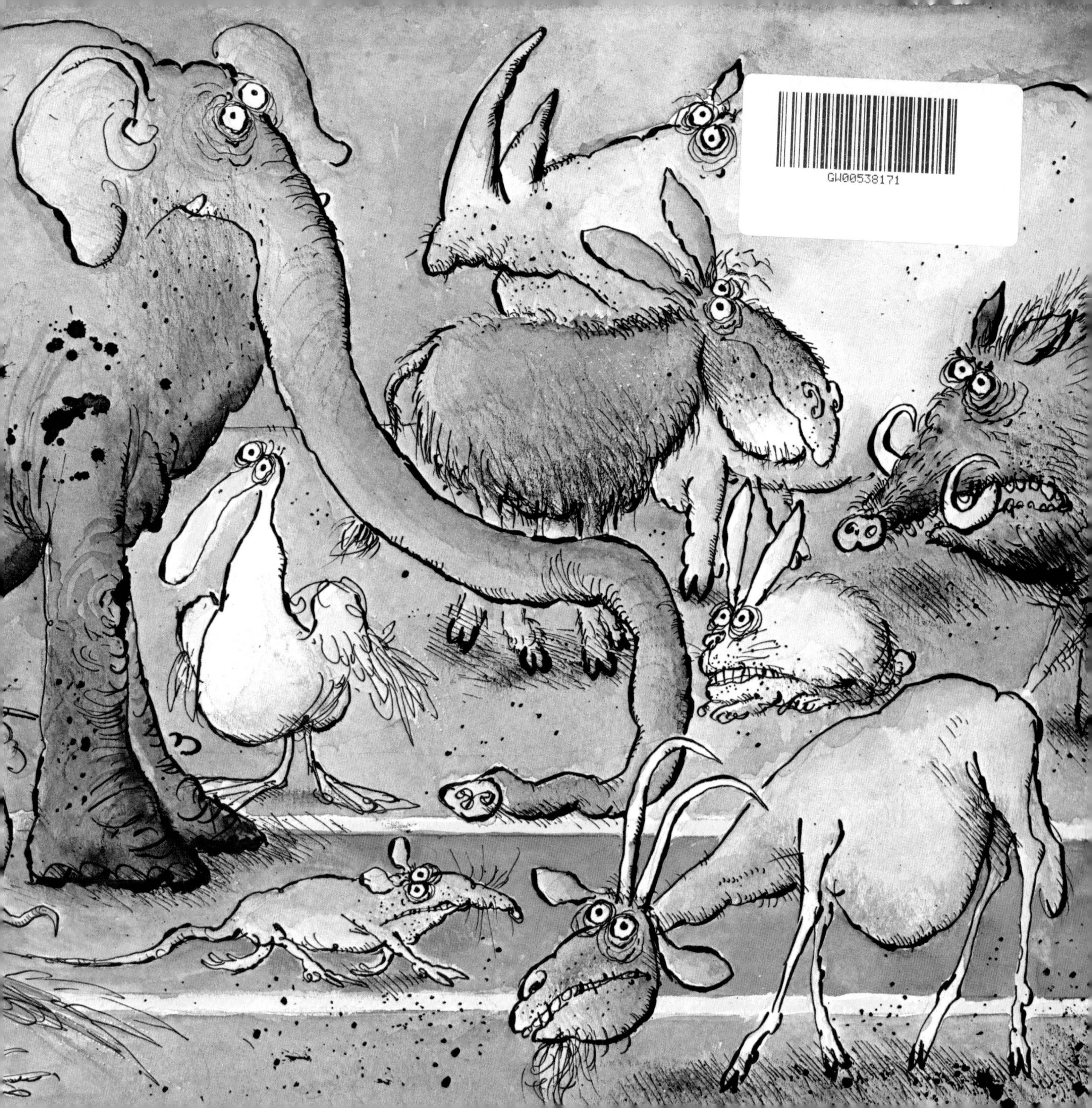

The King of Beasts

& other creatures

RONALD SEARLE

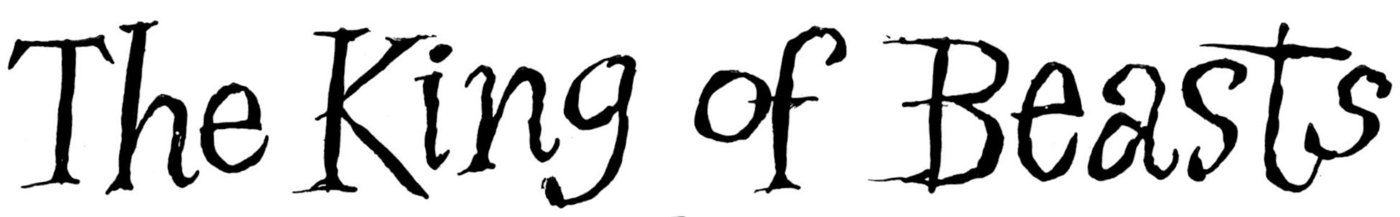

ALLEN LANE

ALLEN LANE
Penguin Books Ltd
536 King's Road
London SW10 0UH

First published 1980

ISBN 0 7139 1336 3

Printed and bound in Great Britain by
William Clowes (Beccles) Limited
Beccles and London

Exhibitionist donkey
about to make an ass of itself

Fastidious rat looking for an
impeccable sewer

Hypersensitive rattlesnake
in search of peace and quiet

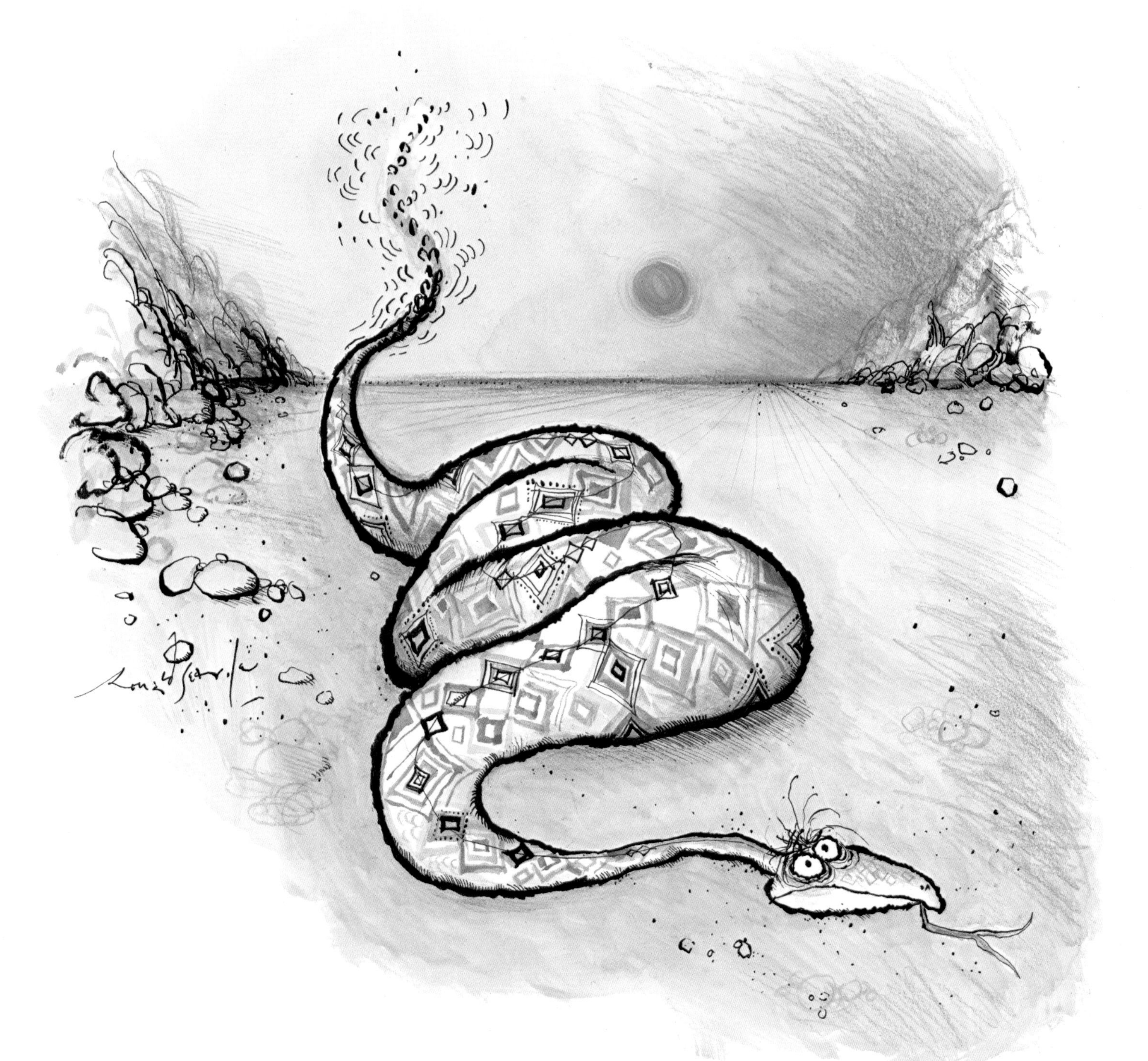

Cretinous owl utterly convinced
that it is revered as a symbol of wisdom

Particularly repellent dog glowing
under the impression that it is man's
best friend

Imbecile rodent confident that
it has a foolproof claim against the
Disney Organization

Loquacious parrot convinced
that it is teaching man a basic vocabulary

Obtuse camel looking for a largish needle

Out-of-touch unicorn unaware that it is a myth

Agnostic serpent attempting to sell apples

Baby seal under the impression
that clubs are centres of social activity

Exceptionally obese hippopotamus
trying to reassure itself that Fat is Fun

Retarded ape happy in the
knowledge that it is the ancestor of Man

American bald eagle suddenly realizing that
its leanings are basically Marxist

E PLURIBUS UNUM

Misinformed crocodile shedding genuine tears

Feeble-minded circus lion basking
in the belief that it is the King of Beasts

Hypochondriac cow going for a cholesterol test

Simple-minded wart-hog reassuring itself
that beauty is more than skin deep

Naïve asp seeking a bosom friend

Hopelessly mixed-up vampire bat
trying to conceal the fact that its tastes
are rigidly vegetarian

Asinine horse thinking that
it is only a question of time before it
replaces the car

Under-sexed double-horned rhinoceros
in search of a reliable aphrodisiac

Muddled sheep in wolf's clothing

Aggressive chicken applying Kung Fu
to a Peking Duck

Conceited egg about to commence its memoirs